IT'S TIME TO LEARN ABOUT BUZZARDS

It's Time to Learn about Buzzards

Walter the Educator

Silent King Books
A WhichHead Entertainment Imprint

Copyright © 2025 by Walter the Educator

All rights reserved. No part of this book may be reproduced in any manner whatsoever without written per- mission except in the case of brief quotations embodied in critical articles and reviews.

First Printing, 2024

Disclaimer

This book is a literary work; the story is not about specific persons, locations, situations, and/or circumstances unless mentioned in a historical context. Any resemblance to real persons, locations, situations, and/or circumstances is coincidental. This book is for entertainment and informational purposes only. The author and publisher offer this information without warranties expressed or implied. No matter the grounds, neither the author nor the publisher will be accountable for any losses, injuries, or other damages caused by the reader's use of this book. The use of this book acknowledges an understanding and acceptance of this disclaimer.

It's Time to Learn about Buzzards is a collectible early learning book by Walter the Educator suitable for all ages belonging to Walter the Educator's Time to Eat Book Series. Collect more books at WaltertheEducator.com

USE THE EXTRA SPACE TO TAKE NOTES AND DOCUMENT YOUR MEMORIES

BUZZARDS

Up in the sky, so high and free,

It's Time to Learn about
Buzzards

A buzzard soars for all to see.

With wings spread wide, it rides the air,

Gliding gently without a care.

It doesn't flap like smaller birds,

It circles high with twists and turns.

Catching breezes, rising tall,

Hardly needing wings at all!

A feathered coat of brown and black,

With a sharp and hooked beak to snack.

Its head is bare, no feathers there,

To keep it clean in open air.

Buzzards do not chase their prey,

They find their meals a different way.

They sniff the air, then swoop on down,

To food that's lying on the ground.

It's Time to Learn about
Buzzards

Some may think that's kind of strange,

But nature works in ways that change.

The buzzard keeps the earth so neat,

By cleaning up what others leave.

With eyesight sharp, it sees so well,

From way up high, it spots the smell.

A helpful bird, so smart and wise,

It cleans the land and clears the skies.

It loves the sun and spreading wings,

To warm itself, oh what a thing!

It perches tall on trees so bare,

And watches all that moves down there.

Buzzards live in nests up high,

On cliffs or trees that touch the sky.

Their babies hatch so soft and small,

It's Time to Learn about
Buzzards

Then grow up strong to soar and call.

Some call them vultures, that is true,

They have a job that they must do.

A tidy helper, big and bold,

The buzzard's tale is one well told.

So when you see one flying by,

With wings spread wide up in the sky,

Remember what the buzzards do,

It's Time to Learn about
Buzzards

They help the world stay clean for you!

ABOUT THE CREATOR

Walter the Educator is one of the pseudonyms for Walter Anderson. Formally educated in Chemistry, Business, and Education, he is an educator, an author, a diverse entrepreneur, and he is the son of a disabled war veteran. "Walter the Educator" shares his time between educating and creating. He holds interests and owns several creative projects that entertain, enlighten, enhance, and educate, hoping to inspire and motivate you. Follow, find new works, and stay up to date with Walter the Educator™

at WaltertheEducator.com

www.ingramcontent.com/pod-product-compliance
Lightning Source LLC
LaVergne TN
LVHW051919060526
838201LV00060B/4081